MILITARY VEHICLES OF THE REICHSWEHR

by Wolfgang Fleischer

Translated from the German by Don Cox

Krupp-Daimler armored cars of the Reichswehr during an exercise in the 1920s.

Schiffer Military/Aviation History
Atglen, PA

Sources and Further Reading:

- BA RH 8/v. 906 (Nr. 766/29 T 2 KKK C 1 g. Kdos. "z" from 24 May 1929, Betr.: E-Programm-Organisationskriegsspiel);
- H.Dv. 471, Handbuch für Kraftfahrer, Berlin 1939, 1942;
- Deiss, W.: Das Deutsche Soldatenbuch, Zweiter Band, Leipzig (no year);
- Ellis, C./Bishop, D.: Transportfahrzeuge des 1. Weltkrieges, Munich 1970
- Felger, F.: Was wir vom Weltkrieg Nicht wissen, Leipzig 1938
- Oswald, W.: Kraftfahrzeuge und Panzer der Reichswehr, Wehrmacht und Bundeswehr, Stuttgart 1990;
- Oswald, W.: Deutsche Autos 1920-1945, Stuttgart 1987;
- Schwarte, M.: Die Technik im Weltkriege, Berlin 1920;
- Spielberger, W.J.: Die Motorisierung der Deutschen Reichswehr 1920-1935, Stuttgart 1979;
- Rabenau, P.: von Seekt-Aus seinem Leben 1918-1936, Leipzig 1940;
- Voss, W. von: Wir vom Verkehr — Die Entwicklung der Preussischen Verkehrstruppen, Berlin 1913;

Photo Credits:

Bundesarchiv (BA) 6, Cayé (CK) 17, Fleischer (WF) 56, Rahne (RH) 2, Militärhistorisches Museum (MHM 2)

Acknowledgments:

The author wishes to thank the following for their assistance in providing material for this volume: Herr Cayé of the Heeresgeschichtlich Militärhistorische Sammlung Holtenau, Frau Riemer, Frau Wetzig and Herr Thiede — all from the Militärhistorisches Museum Dresden.

Krupp-Daimler Geuschützkraftwagen Kw. 19 in firing position. (WF)

Copyright © 1996 by Schiffer Publishing, Ltd.

Printed in China.
ISBN: 0-7643-0166-7
This book was originally published under the title,
Waffen Arsenal-Heeresübliche Kraftfahrzeuge Und Anhänger Der Reichswehr
by Podzun-Pallas Verlag

We are interested in hearing from authors with book ideas on related topics.

Published by Schiffer Publishing Ltd.
77 Lower Valley Road
Atglen, PA 19310
Please write for a free catalog.
This book may be purchased from the publisher.
Please include $2.95 postage.
Try your bookstore first.

Testing of army cargo transports by the Versuchsabteilung of the Verkehrstruppe. By 1907 158 various transport types had been tested and permitted as subsidy-approved vehicles. It wasn't until 1908 that the requirements increased by any significant amount.

In Germany, the idea of using motor vehicles for military purposes was not enthusiastically welcomed prior to World War One. It was only after lengthy testing by the Versuchsabteilung (Research Dept.) of the Verkehrstruppe that specialized army vehicles were developed which could move a 6-ton load (carried on both the tractor and trailer together). Yet at the same time these vehicles were able to reach speeds of 8-12 kilometers per hour. As a comparison: a Proviantwagen 05 heavy supply wagon could only be loaded with 1.2 tons; pulled by a team of four horses, it had an average road speed of 6 kilometers per hour. The advantage was clearly with the motor-driven vehicles. Despite this, "motorized" didn't replace "horse-drawn." The situation was only partially alleviated by providing subsidies of several thousand marks to companies on the economy which had transport vehicles in their inventories that met the requirements of the Verkehrstruppe. By this arrangement the vehicles would be handed over to the Vehrkehrstruppe in case of war. On 1 October 1911 there were 611 subsidy vehicles available. Though this number rose by the time the First World War broke out, it was certainly not sufficient to play a greater role in the rising transportation needs of the Army. The railroad and horse-drawn vehicles carried an incomparably greater quantity of materiel. Basically, however, motorized vehicle units were able to prove their worth during the course of the First World War, although the oversights made during the prewar period were never fully redressed.

The use of personnel vehicles was in a similar state of affairs. Here, however, there was no specialized design and the large percentage of requisitioned civilian vehicles were not suited for military purposes.

Interesting developments in the area of specialized motor-driven artillery transports for the Army's heavy artillery pieces occurred during the war. All told, the motorization of Germany's army never reached the comparatively high levels enjoyed by the armed forces of England and France. Crises in the industry, raw material and work force shortages all played their part in widening the parity gap once it had been established.

After Germany's defeat in the First World War efforts were undertaken to evaluate the experience gathered by the Verkehrstruppe; the mistakes of the pre-war era were not to be repeated. The work, however, was hampered by the regulations of the Versailles Treaty. Vehicle inventory was reduced considerably. Development and production of modern all-terrain and armored vehicles was either restricted or banned outright. The victorious Allies, primarily France, closely supervised the adherence to the treaty's accords. In addition, on 15 September 1919 the Inter-Allied Military Control Commission began its work. It could — at any time and without prior announcement — carry out factory inspections. For the Germans, this meant that there would be few four-wheel drive or armor vehicles and tanks were out of the question altogether. New developments were constantly being blocked and had to be undertaken under the strictest secrecy.

The Inspektion der Kraftfahrtruppen (Inspection of Motorized Troops) was established under the Reichswehr. For a time this organization even included both motorized and horse-drawn supply units. There were seven motorized units, one for each infantry division in the Army. As a side note, the future

Soldiers of the II Battalion, Infanterieregiment 464 being transported in the vicinity of Arras. Photo taken in the summer of 1917. With the aid of motorized vehicle convoys fresh troops could be thrown relatively quickly into front-line areas threatened by enemy forces. (WF)

The German Army operated 12,000 personnel carriers at the high point of motorized vehicle expansion — here, a 10/30 PS NSU. (WF)

Generaloberst Heinz Guderian, who became the Generalinspekteur der Panzertruppe in 1943, served as a Hauptmann in 1922 in the 7th (bayrische) Kraftfahrabteilung.

In order to (theoretically) keep abreast of international developments in the area of army motorization, considerable weight was given to articles in foreign military journals, subject-matter literature and trade publications. And naturally efforts continued to be made in the area of vehicle development at home. Prototypes of all-terrain and armored vehicles appeared. The Chef der Heeresleitung (Chief of Army Command) at the time, Generaloberst von Seekt, framed the thinking of this period in some basic considerations for the rebuilding of the Wehrmacht. In the early 1920s, Seekt wrote: "Weapons technology is to be promoted through the application of science which balances technical perfection with quantity and training. An alliance with technology and industry is to be forged and maintained." A typical example demonstrating the realization of this concept is the Reichswehr's first motorization program, implemented in 1926. Within the guidelines established by this program, well-known companies were awarded contracts for the development of heavy personnel carriers, light cargo trucks with 1.5-ton and heavy cargo trucks with 3.0-ton capacities. Over the next few years approximately 6000 1.5 tonners were built by Mercedes-Benz, Büssing-NAG and Magirus. The Heereswaffenamt (Army Weapons Office) entrusted the design and production of the 6-wheel all-terrain 3-ton class to the companies of Henschel, Büssing-NAG and Krupp. Mercedes-Benz was also included later.

In an "organizational war game" (the cover term given to the development program of the Reichswehr's Truppenamt) from 24 May 1929 the fundamental stipulations were spelled out in the area of Army motorization: "Unification and simplification with regard to production and use.

Berlin, March 1920. Troops of the Marinebrigade roll through the streets during the Kapp-Lüttwitz putsch. The front axle of this 3-ton Army transport is fitted with sprung steel wheels, a result of the acute shortage of rubber tires in Germany during the First World War which carried over into the postwar period. (WF)

Two armored cars of improvised construction based on cargo transport chassis, being used by Freikorps troops. The combat value of such vehicles, which as a rule were fitted with untempered steel sheeting, remained low. Their existence stimulated the Reichswehr into creating armored wheeled vehicles; just as critical, though, was the analysis of operational experience. (WF)

Another form of improvised armored car design, March 1920 in Berlin's Potsdamer Strasse. (WF)

The Reichswehr's motorized units often practiced moving infantry and artillery units during exercises. Photo taken during the latter half of the 1920s.

- As far as possible, use of peace-time economy equipment with a view to the raw material situation and the absence of
- specialized equipment
- confined to the most critical and important developments."

During the latter half of the 1920s the following points were crystallized:

1. The acquisition of theoretical foundations in organization, technology and tactics of motorized troop operations. Both indigenous and foreign experience was utilized. The findings of this effort were published and discussed in trade journals and literature.

2. Basic research, developmental work and tests in the sub-elements of the motorized vehicle industry. This affected such areas as: fuels and lubricants, engine and drive units, brakes, suspension, tires, etc. One example: according to the postal log of the Inspektion für Waffen und Gerät (Inspection Office for Weapons and Equipment) in January of 1928 tires were delivered from Vorwerk & Sohn/Barman for testing in Kummersdorf-Schiessplatz.

3. The selection, testing and (in cases of suitability) acquisition of civilian vehicles from the economy. An example of this is the acquisition of Hanomag industrial tractors for the Reichswehr. These vehicles soldiered on, pulling Pf 12 pontoon vehicles with bridge-laying units, up until the end of the 1930s.

4. The design of specialized vehicles. In the developmental program of 1929 it stated: "In the situation were no alternative means can be found for motorized transportation of heavy artillery and anti-aircraft guns heavy transports must be developed." Similar requirements were laid out for the development of specialized vehicles for fire-control, aircraft acquisition, tank identification and acoustics measuring equipment. All extremely valuable pieces of equipment, the use of which was linked to a high degree of mobility and reliability.

5. The development of armored wheeled vehicles for reconnaissance and command applications. This was a new generation of vehicles, born with the creation of the mittlerer Personenkraftwagen (4 x 2) Adler Standard 6 and the schwerer Panzerspähwagen (6 x 4), produced by Mercedes-Benz (the G 3 a(p)), Büssing-NAG (as the G 31 (p)) and Magirus (as the M 206 (p)). The development of tank mockups on vehicles was also unique.

6. The development of various specialized trailers, including those for searchlights, engineering equipment, etc.

The following distinctions were made with regard to vehicle classes used in the Reichswehr:

1. personnel and light vehicles
2. ambulances
3. omnibuses
4. cargo transports

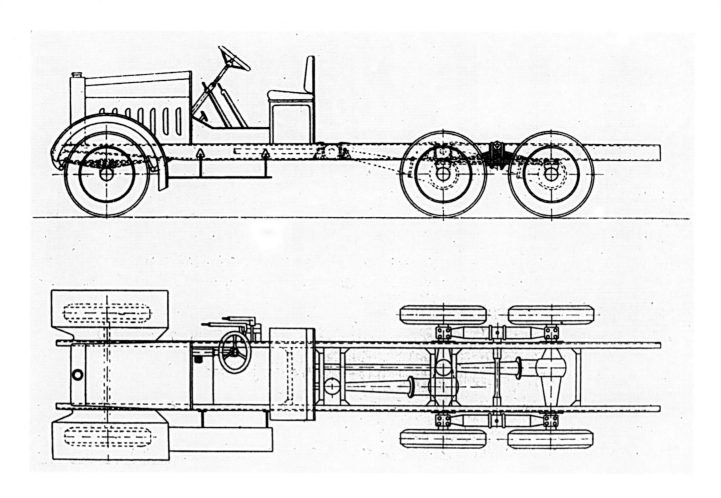

The chassis of a three-axle vehicle designed by Büssing-NAG. This basic drawing was taken from the "Handbuch für Kraftfahrer", compiled and published in 1928 by the Reichswehrministerium, Inspektion für Waffen und Gerät. (WF)

5. trailers (including field kitchens, illumination and fuel trailers)
6. motorcycles
7. tractors/transports
8. specialized artillery vehicles
9. specialized vehicles for the communications branch
    a. omnibus type
    b. standard cargo transport type
10. armored vehicles

The "Bilderatlas der heeresüblichen Kraftfahrzeuge nebst Charakteristik (Picture Atlas of Common Army Vehicles Including Characteristics, a supplement to Wehramt Nr. 6350/32 g. Kdos. St.A.N. from 1 December 1932)" is an excellent source for an overview of the state of development achieved by the end of 1932 in the area of Army motorization. According to this publication, by that time important prerequisites had been set in the area of powered vehicle technology that, in turn, were able to meet the requirements of the Reichswehr. Although the circumstances which accompanied the lengthy developmental process did not necessarily permit the most ideal solutions (such as all-wheel drive, four-wheel steering, etc.), at least the shape of the Reichswehr's future motorized vehicle program became discernible. To be sure, the Versailles Treaty and its restrictions had a negative influence on the concrete development work and acquisition of vehicles. On the other hand, it was initially possible to observe developments in the motorized vehicle industry and then make decisions based on modern solutions. New concepts had to be established in any case; the Reichswehr had little in the way of vehicle stocks that would have justified continued support. This resulted in a significant qualitative difference when compared with the victorious nations of World War One, which, like France, were forced to make use of their large pre-1919 vehicle stockpiles all the way until the end of the 1930s.

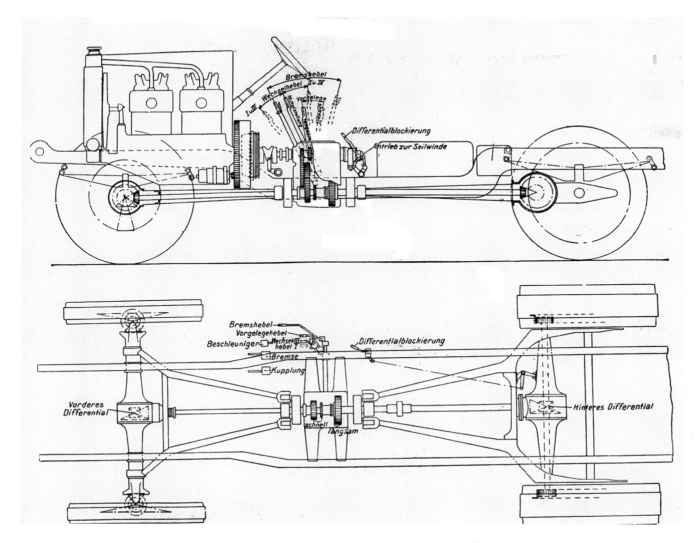

Schematic diagram of a four-wheel drive vehicle, designed during the first half of the 1920s. (WF)

Left:
In addition to evaluating all problems associated with maintenance, the Heereswaffenamt, Inspektion für Waffen und Gerät conducted thorough research and testing for determining the most effective types of tires and shape for military vehicles. (WF)

Below:
The Hanomag industrial tractor. Vehicles of this type served in the private sector for towing trailers on paved roads. They were cheap to produce and found use in the Reichswehr with motorized bridge-laying units. (WF)

Right: Front view of the Gefrat Kettenschlepper(tracked tractor), a development concept popular in the mid-1920s. (WF)

The Heereswaffenamt, Inspektion für Waffen und Gerät, analyzed various wheeled and tracked tractors from both indigenous and foreign sources. The latter often made rather adventurous journeys to get to Germany. The Kettenschlepper shown in the picture carries the unrevealing name of Gefrat (= Gesellschaft für Frachttransport, or Corporation for Freight Transport). It bears a strong resemblance to the Russian tractors of the 1930s. (WF)

Right:
The Adler-Favorit was procured by the Reichswehr in small numbers between 1929 and 1932. The four-cylinder engine produced 35 hp. (CK)

Above and below: The Wanderer W 11 was produced from 1933 on and acquitted itself well in operational use. 2844 vehicles were manufactured. These were used as command cars and in anti-tank companies of infantry regiments as tow vehicles for the 3.7 cm Pak L/45. (WF)

In 1926 the Reichswehr obtained a small quantity of six-wheeled all-terrain vehicles, including five Horch 8s. Gross weight was 4680 kg and an 8-cylinder Horch engine with 80 hp powered it, giving the vehicle a maximum speed of 70 kmh. (CK)

Right:
Additional developments of the six-wheeled all-terrain vehicle were made by Daimler-Benz (in the form of the G 1 and G 3) and the Selve Automobilwerken AG in Hamelin. The G 3 shown in the picture was based on the 1.5-ton cargo transport chassis. (BA)

Above: The Horch 8 Type 350 was delivered in small numbers as the Kfz. 21 heavy all-terrain personnel carrier. It had four-wheel drive, an 80 hp engine and could carry 5-6 men.

Left page: One of the first Wanderer W 11 command vehicles. The spare tires were carried at the rear. Officially, it was called the mittlerer geländegängiger Personenkraftwagen Kfz. 11(medium all-terrain personnel carrier). It had four bucket seats, an adjustable windscreen with side screens and a collapsible cover. When designated Kfz. 12 the vehicle was fitted with a tow assembly for the 3.7 cm Pak L/45 and the Sd. Anh. 32 (WF)

Right: The Horch six-wheeled all-terrain vehicle offered sufficient space for up to six men. (CK)

The Kfz. 31 ambulance. Characteristics of this vehicle, for which several types of commonly available cargo transports were used, were an enclosed body with windows, side and rear doors and luggage rack. The interior layout varied depending upon use. (WF)

A telegraph position (motorized) in operation. The Kfz. 61 telegraph vehicle was built from the Mercedes-Benz G 3a, Büssing-NAG G 31 and Magirus M 206 light all-terrain transports. (WF)

A Mercedes-Benz G 3a 1.5-ton (6x4) light all-terrain transport as a Kfz. 61 light radio vehicle. General features of the Kfz. 61 were an enclosed box superstructure with windows and doors. The interior varied with use. (WF)

Vehicles of an artillery observation battalion prior to moving out on maneuvers. Included in the photo are four Kfz. 61s. (WF)

Below: Henschel 33 D 1, Krupp L 3 H 63 and Büssing-NAG GL 6 medium all-terrain cargo transports were used as the basis for the Kfz. 74 anti-aircraft range finding/plane spotting troop carriers. General characteristics were an open bed with hoops and tarpaulins, two longitudinal benches and attachments for carrying replacement parts to the command equipment. (WF)

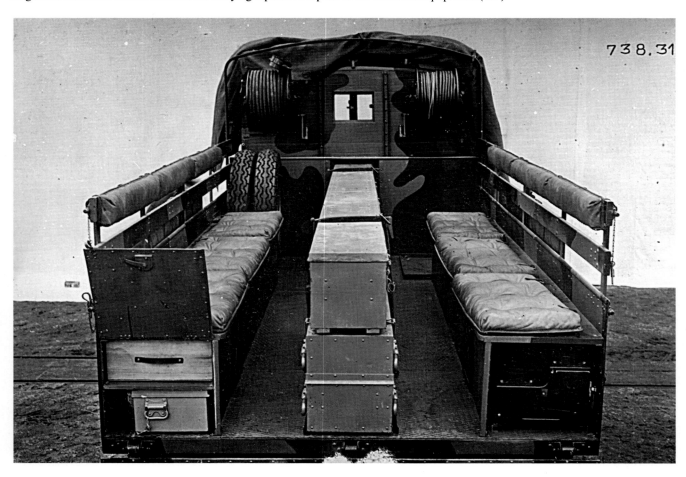

We are the motorized troops! There was no lack of self confidence among the specialists of the Reichswehr's motorized battalions. Scrapbook photo of an exercise, 1929. (CK)

Later, in the vehicle registry list for cargo transports of the Wehrmacht, it no longer appeared — the Kfz. 75 engine transport. General features were an open bed with equipment for transporting aircraft engines and a crane for on- and off-loading. The vehicle was a Büssing-NAG Typ 3 GL 6. (WF)

As of 15 March 1933 the Kfz. 73 was listed as the survey troop vehicle, here built upon a Krupp L 3 H 63 medium all-terrain cargo truck. The specialized superstructure housing had seats forward for the personnel, while in the rear were lockable boxes for the equipment. (WF)

136.30

Taking a break during driving school. In addition to acquiring suitable vehicles the Reichswehr placed great emphasis on comprehensive training for personnel showing aptitude as drivers. (CK)

A total of 15 different application types were found for the Kfz. 72. These included a command vehicle, a weather vehicle and a radio intercept truck. The enclosed box body with windows and doors could be configured in a variety of ways, depending upon requirements. (WF)

A large number of Henschel Typ 33 D1 6x4 medium all-terrain trucks were produced between 1933 and 1941. This photo was taken in the latter half of the 1930s. (MHM)

Already belonging to the class of veterans in 1941 — the Henschel 33 B 1, built in appreciable quantity for the Reichswehr between 1928 and 1934. Photo from July 1941, Eastern Front. (WF)

Some of the features common to the Kfz. 51 mobile machine shop were an enclosed specialized body with side walls that could be raised for expanding the work space. It was suitable for setting up machinery and workbenches (based on needs). Subtypes included a communications mobile machine shop and an aircraft mobile machine shop. (WF above, CK below)

Locations of Motorized Troop Units in Germany 1927

1 = Königsberg	10 = Kassel
2 = Allenstein	11 = Leipzig
3 = Kolberg	12 = Dresden
4 = Stettin	13 = Neisse
5 = Schwerin	14 = Würzburg
6 = Berlin-Lankwitz	15 = Fürth
7 = Magdeburg	16 = Stuttgart-Cannstatt
8 = Hannover	17 = Ulm
9 = Münster	18 = Munich

Above and below: Maneuver photos from the early 1930s. The drivers wore leather clothing, a protective helmet made of leather and protective goggles. (CK)

The Krupp-Daimler prime mover was delivered as the Sd. Kfz. 2 having an open superstructure with braces and tarpaulin for personnel and equipment. It had four-wheel drive, a winch and a trailer hitch. (WF)

Above and below: The motorized gun batteries also found use for the KD-1 prime movers as ammunition transporters and recovery vehicles.

The Kraftwagen 19 as a motorized gun platform (self-propelled) (Kw 19 als Gesch. Kw.) was listed as the Sd. Kfz. 1. It had an open superstructure and was suitable for carrying a 7.5 cm anti-aircraft gun (Kraftwagengeschütz 14) in a socket carriage with its crew and ammunition. (WF)

A motorized gun platform weighed 11.25 tons. Each vehicle had a crew of nine men. Each motorized gun battery comprised four Sd. Kfz. 1s. (CK)

Below: Setting out for firing training. Notice the cable winch in its stabile road-travel position and the shape of the all-rubber tires.

On the basis of a writ from the Wehramt of the Reichswehr, dated 25 March 1929, plans were made to refit the barrels of 120 anti-aircraft guns from 7.7 cm to 7.5 cm during the time period from 1930 to 1932. Of these, 80 were planned for the Kraftwagen 19 (Sd. Kfz. 1) gun platforms. Only 28 were permitted to be officially carried out. (CK)

The mobile gun platforms were considered extremely valuable assets, since they were both mobile and effective as a means of defense against aircraft and tanks. They could fire the 7.5 cm standard round and the 7.5 cm shell with armor-piercing cap and tracer. (CK)

The Reichswehr used the specialized Krupp-Daimler chassis under the designation of Sd. Kfz. 3 armored vehicle, equipped with additional rearward steering. The enclosed armored body was able to withstand impacts from 7.92 cm pointed bullets. It had viewports and hatches (the latter having mounts for machine guns). It could transport 12 men — or 6 men with machine guns. (WF)

Right:
The Reichswehr was permitted to have 105 armored vehicles (15 for each division). Because of their limited combat value, however, only 45 were acquired — either through modification or new design. The mount attachments for four heavy machine guns had to be hidden from the eyes of the Inter-Allied Control Commission. (WF)

In 1927 and 1928 trials were conducted with medium-wave radios in armored cars. The 20-watt transmitter had a range of 5000 meters when transmitting voice signals and 15000 meters when transmitting wireless telegraph signals. (WF)

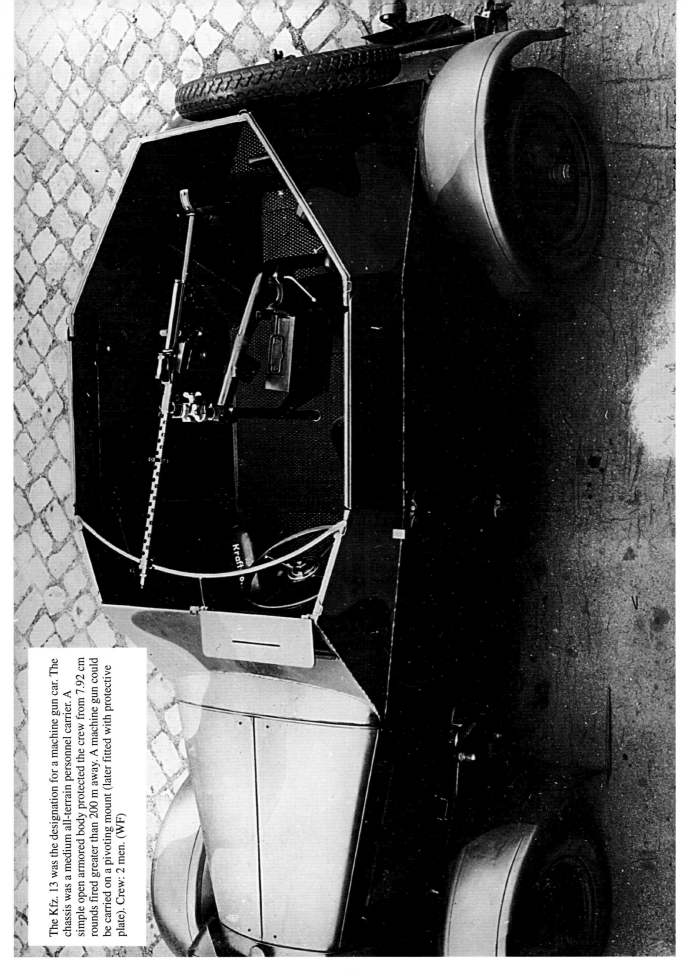

The Kfz. 13 was the designation for a machine gun car. The chassis was a medium all-terrain personnel carrier. A simple open armored body protected the crew from 7.92 cm rounds fired greater than 200 m away. A machine gun could be carried on a pivoting mount (later fitted with protective plate). Crew: 2 men. (WF)

By 1934 Daimler-Benz in Berlin-Marienfelde had produced 147 Kfz. 13 machine-gun cars and an additional 40 Kfz. 14 communications cars. They provided valuable service during the expansion of the armored reconnaissance battalions and were still in operational use in 1939. (WF)

Approximately 1000 Kfz. 67 armored cars and Kfz. 67 a radio command cars (later Sd. Kfz. 231 and 232) were procured for the armored reconnaissance troops between 1930 and 1936. Photo is of a Kfz. 67 a armored command car. (WF)

590/32

The Kfz. 67 armored car was designed from the chassis of the Daimler-Benz, Büssing-NAG and Magirus light all-terrain trucks. It had an enclosed armored body designed to withstand 7.92 mm pointed steel-core armor-piercing rounds and a turret. As of 15 March 1933 the vehicle was fitted with a 2 cm heavy machine gun and an MG 13. (WF)

Above and below: Tank mockups based on personnel carrier chassis played a particularly important training role in the Reichswehr. Representative of the many, sometimes improvised tank dummies are the mockups shown here based on the Adler "Standard 6." They had a four-man crew and were produced from 1930 onward. (both BA)

TRAILERS

Specialized trailers(Sonderanhänger, or Sd. Ah.) were given special emphasis in the Reichswehr's motorization program. The photograph shows an Sd. Ah. 32 being towed by a Kfz. 12 medium personnel carrier with shock-absorbed trailer hitch. The Sd. Ah. 32 served as an ammunition carrier for the 3.7 cm Tak (3.7 cm Tankabwehrkanone, later the 3.7 cm Panzerabwehrkanone L/45). (WF)

The Sd. Ah. 21 single-axle trailer for telegraph work was used by communications units. A light housing was fitted with four storage compartments and a tool box, all able to carry telegraph installation equipment. (WF)

The Sd. Ah. 1 was used by motorized artillery battalions, which were initially forced to make use of guns designed to be pulled by horse-drawn teams. The trailer was characterized as a single-axle for light and medium guns, had an open superstructure with attachments for loading and securing the guns. It was towed by light or medium all-terrain cargo trucks. (WF)

Not yet given the standard trailer number by 15 March 1933 — 110 V (16.5 kW) power generator, which served with anti-aircraft units as a power supply for the 110 cm searchlight. The power generator was fixed to the frame and protected by side-lifting sheet metal panels. Medium trucks provided the tow. The 220 V power generator was similar, being used by artillery observation units. (WF)

Numbered among the Army's common trailers was the Sd. Ah. 2, which was a single-axle trailer used by anti-aircraft units for the 110 cm searchlight. Features: open specialized superstructure, forked frame, suitable for loading a 110 cm searchlight and having three storage compartments. (WF)

K.128c-33

The Ah. 13 (trailer, single-axle) was used to carry motor boats by motorized and semi-motorized engineer bridge-laying units. It had an open frame design with equipment for loading and releasing a motorboat. (WF)

In addition to the Ah. 13 the Sd. Ah. 14 and the Sd. Ah. 111 and 112 were used by bridge-laying engineers for pontoon bridge equipment. (WF)

A Büssing-NAG Typ 3 GL 6 6x4 3-ton medium all-terrain cargo truck with an Sd. Ah. 14 attached. Engineers are standing by, waiting to offload the bridging equipment and assemble the bridge approach. (WF)

An Sd. Ah. 14 trailer for bridging equipment. The single-axle chassis with double tires had a low-hung drop frame with attachments for loading and securing bridge-laying equipment. Beneath the frame was a compartment for accessories and supplies. (WF)

The Ah. 51 illumination trailer was a 2.5-ton trailer having an enclosed box design with an interior layout to accommodate a power supply, batter charger and illumination equipment. The design resembled that of the Kfz. 41 (illumination vehicle) and the Kfz. 51 (mobile repair shop). (WF)

MOTORCYCLES

Motorcycles were cheap to build and maintain and therefore, with their barely measurable cost, played an important role in the Reichswehr. Training of the soldiers was intense and wasn't without its mishaps, as seen in the photo here. (CK)

The motorcycle inventory was quite diverse. The Victoria, BMW, Zündapp and NSU makes were all represented. Even the light motor-bikes of DKW (the photo shows the forerunner of the DKW RT 125) were utilized as liaison and communication motorcycles. (CK)

The Spielberger German Armor & Military Vehicles Series

Four volumes in the classic series by reknowned German panzer historian Walter Spielberger are now available English editions. Known for his emphasis on detail, Spielberger chronicles each production variation and later mo tions. Line drawings by Hilary Doyle complement the discussion of each model type.

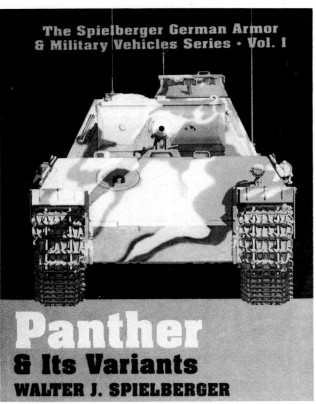

Size: 8 1/2" x 11" 288 pages hard cover
over 460 photographs
ISBN: 0-88740-397-2 $39.95

Size: 8 1/2" x 11" 256 pages hard cover
over 240 photographs
ISBN: 0-88740-398-0 $39.95

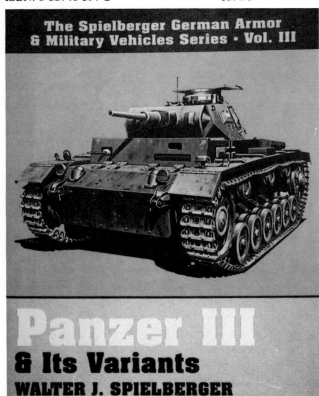

Size: 8 1/2" x 11" 168 pages hard cover
over 200 photographs
ISBN: 0-88740-448-0 $29.95

Size: 8 1/2" x 11" 168 pages hard cover
over 200 photographs
ISBN: 0-88740-515-0 $29.95